I Love Sports

Football

by Allan Morey

Bullfrog Books

Ideas for Parents and Teachers

Bullfrog Books let children practice reading informational text at the earliest reading levels. Repetition, familiar words, and photo labels support early readers.

Before Reading

- Discuss the cover photo. What does it tell them?
- Look at the picture glossary together. Read and discuss the words.

Read the Book

- "Walk" through the book and look at the photos. Let the child ask questions. Point out the photo labels.
- Read the book to the child, or have him or her read independently.

After Reading

- Prompt the child to think more. Ask: Have you played football before? Have you watched a game? What did each player do?

Bullfrog Books are published by Jump!
5357 Penn Avenue South
Minneapolis, MN 55419
www.jumplibrary.com

Library of Congress Cataloging-in-Publication Data

Morey, Allan.
  Football / by Allan Morey.
    pages cm. — (I love sports)
  Summary: "This photo-illustrated book for early readers introduces the basics of football and encourages kids to try it. Includes labeled diagram of football field and photo glossary." — Provided by publisher.
  Includes bibliographical references and index.
  Audience: Age: 5.
  Audience: Grade: K to Grade 3.
  ISBN 978-1-62031-178-3 (hardcover) —
  ISBN 978-1-62496-265-3 (ebook)
  1. Football for children—Juvenile literature.
  I. Title.
  GV959.55.C45H64 2015
  796.332—dc23
                                   2014031357

Series Editor: Rebecca Glaser
Series Designer: Ellen Huber
Book Designer: Anna Peterson
Photo Researcher: Anna Peterson

Photo Credits: All photos by Shutterstock except: Alamy, 6–7, 23ml; Corbis, 5; Dreamstime, 8–9; Getty, 10–11, 16, 19, 23mr; iStock, cover, 18–19, 23bl; Thinkstock, 1, 3, 4, 12–13, 14, 17, 23tl, 23tr, 23br.

Printed in the United States of America at Corporate Graphics in North Mankato, Minnesota.

Table of Contents

Let's Play Football! 4

At the Football Field 22

Picture Glossary 23

Index 24

To Learn More 24

Let's Play Football!

Grab a ball. Put on your helmet and pads.

It is time to play!

The Jets have the ball.
Ted is their quarterback.
He yells, "Hike!"

quarterback

The quarterback
throws the ball.

Lisa catches it.

Now Sam has the ball.

He runs right.

He runs left.

The other team tries
to stop the runner.

Bart dives.

He tackles the runner.

Ali gets the ball.

She runs into
the end zone.

end
zone

Touchdown! Six points!

Dina kicks the ball.

It goes to the other team.

Now the Bills try to score.

The team with the most points wins.

Would you like to play?

Catch a ball.

Football is fun!

At the Football Field

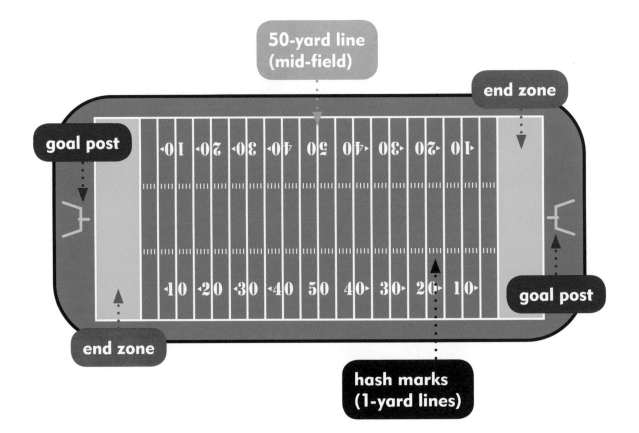

50-yard line (mid-field)

end zone

goal post

end zone

goal post

hash marks (1-yard lines)

Picture Glossary

pads
Protective equipment worn under a player's uniform to prevent injury.

tackle
To knock down another player to stop him or her from scoring.

quarterback
The player on a football team who throws the ball or hands off the ball to a runner.

team
A group of players who play together; there are 11 players on a football team.

runner
Any player who runs with the football to try to score.

touchdown
A score in football worth six points, scored when a player has the ball in the other team's end zone.

Index

end zone 14

helmet 4

kicking 16

pads 4

quarterback 6, 8

runner 13

scoring 19

tackle 13

team 13, 17, 19

touchdown 15

To Learn More

Learning more is as easy as 1, 2, 3.

1) Go to www.factsurfer.com

2) Enter "football" into the search box.

3) Click the "Surf" button to see a list of websites.

With factsurfer.com, finding more information is just a click away.

5/17 ② 8/16